Gosforth
Remembered

Central Park, Gosforth. 11956

by Andrew Clark & George Nairn

One of Gosforth's most famous exports. Greggs on Gosforth High Street today and an advert from when the company was known as 'Greggs of Gosforth'. It was in Gosforth in 1951 that the firm, which is now a multi-million company with shops nationwide, began life.

Previous page: A postcard of the bandstand in Gosforth Central Park. Today, the Gosforth War Memorial Pillar stands on the site of the bandstand (see page 25). Fully grown trees now line the path.

Front cover top right: American-born Colonel Cody in his aeroplane at Gosforth during the Daily Mail Circuit of Britain Air Race in July 1911 (see page 16).

Top left: Lilian Langley, proprietor of Langley Brothers Dairymen, South Gosforth on a family day out to Alnmouth in 1935.

Bottom: Gosforth High Street around the time of the First World War.

Back cover, top: The gates of Gosforth Park around 1934.

Bottom: Haddricks Mill Road, South Gosforth in the 1920s.

Copyright Andrew Clark & George Nairn 2017

First published in 2017 by

Summerhill Books
PO Box 1210, Newcastle-upon-Tyne NE99 4AH

www.summerhillbooks.co.uk

email: summerhillbooks@yahoo.co.uk

ISBN: 978-1-911385-13-4

No part of this publication may be reproduced, stored in a mechanical retrieval system, or transmitted, in any form or by any means, electronic, mechanical, photocopying, recording or otherwise, without prior permission of the authors.

Contents

Gosforth Parish Church of St Nicholas, around 1900. There was been a church on this site for hundreds of years with the present building dating from 1799.

An aerial view of Gosforth Park Hotel in 1966, a year after its opening.

One of the more unusual visitors to the Stable Bar at the Gosforth Park Hotel in the early 1970s.

Acknowledgements

The authors would like to thank the following who have kindly helped with this book:

Alan Brett, John Brett, Harry & Pauline Clark, Philip Curtis, Sharyn Taylor

Beamish Museum – The North of England Open Air Museum
The Chronicle
The Journal
Sunderland Echo

Bibliography

Evening Chronicle
Newcastle Journal
Northern Football
Morpeth Herald
Sunday Sun
Sunderland Daily Echo
Up North Combine Handbook, 1955
The Pitman's Derby by Mike Kirkup
Played in Tyne and Wear by Lynn Pearson
Kelly's Directory of Northumberland
Ward's Directory of Newcastle
Remarkable Events, Connected with the Borough of Gateshead

Introduction

Gosforth has a fascinating history and it is recalled in the following pages with over 150 picture postcards, archive photographs and old advertisements. We start with postcards, many from over a century ago, that take us on a tour of the High Street. Alongside them are some 'then and now' images to show how things have changed over the past hundred years. Other old postcards (such as the one on the right of Salters Road) are also included and show nearby streets, buildings, local businesses and people.

There are also stories of Gosforth's history – coal mining in the area; Gosforth in the two World Wars; Gosforth Park Racecourse and the Northumberland Plate.

The everyday life of Gosforth is featured with photographs of local pubs, cinemas, hospitals, transport and sport.

Dipping into the area's more unusual history we tell the stories of when the Daily Mail Circuit of Britain Air Race came to Gosforth in 1911 and when the Suffragettes campaigning for Votes for Women attacked the Globe Cinema and Gosforth Golf Club.

All these stories and more are just of a glimpse of Gosforth's rich heritage and we hope you enjoy this book.

Andrew Clark
Summerhill Books, 2017

Gosforth High Street around 1910. A loaded cart stands in front of one of the shops. It looks like the man beside the cart, wearing the apron, is scratching his head. Is there a problem with the delivery? On the right, a smartly dressed girl waits at the stop for the approaching tram.

Moor Edge

A view of 'Moor End' showing the Little Bridge over the Craghall Burn that was once the old boundary between Gosforth and Newcastle. Gosforth became part of Newcastle in 1974 as part of the massive re-organisation of local government throughout the country.

A postcard of Moor Edge from around 1930. It's a busy scene with a car, delivery van, wagon and horse and cart making their way towards Gosforth. On the left are seats that were said to be a popular spot for nannies from local houses to meet while out with the children in their care.

Moor Edge eight-five years after the postcard above. This busy road now needs a pedestrian crossing and trees obscure the view of the houses on the left. The seats still remain – nice to see somethings do not change.

The High Street

The High Street looking north around 1935. On the left is Eveline A. Layburne's tobacconists and confectioners. This postcard was published by Robert Johnston of Gateshead who was one of the best photographers of the era. Another of his postcards is on page 9 (middle image) and that photograph was taken on the same day over eighty years ago.

High Street, Gosforth. 8976

The High Street in 2017. Eveline A. Layburne's shop is long gone and Ciel School Uniform is in its place. The building now has a new floor above the shop. It is good that this part of the High Street is still popular with shoppers.

The High Street looking south before the First World War. On the right is a branch of the North Eastern Bank at Number 17. The manager in 1911 was Mr W. Hendry. The North Eastern Banking group was later taken over by Martins Bank Limited who merged with Barclays in 1969. Today this bank is still a branch of Barclays.

The High Street around the time of the First World War. On the far left is Tyler & Sons boot dealers then an impressive looking Boots the Chemist with a sign saying 'Prescriptions Carefully Dispensed'. Next door is the post office – providing vital communication links at a time when few people had telephones and telegrams were the quickest way to send messages. Two telegraph boys wait

by the side of the road with one checking his bike. The boys are standing in front of William Moore's the Undertaker.

The High Street around 1905. The County Inn at Number 75 is on the right – now a Grade II listed building. Before the First World War the County was owned by James Deuchar Ltd which ran a number of north east pubs and supplied Lochside Beers from their brewery in Montrose.

Over a hundred years later and the County is still a popular local pub that has survived the many closures suffered by other drinking establishments. Today, people enjoy drinking outside and a number of people in the photograph are doing this – a way of drinking that was unheard of at the time of the image above.

The High Street around 1920. The Number 8 tram is on its way to the Central Station. This popular form of transport disappeared from local streets in 1950. On the right, by the tram is the Central Buildings that houses a number of shops.

HIGH STREET, GOSFORTH.

High Street, Gosforth. 8973

Left: The view a little further along the High Street than the previous postcard, this time around 1935. The shops of the Central Buildings now have awnings. The shop second from the right is the Buttercup Dairy Company and is advertising butter and tea on its awning.

Below left: Eighty years later and a bus has replaced the tram as the main form of public transport on the High Street. The awnings have gone from the shops on the right while behind the bus is the Gosforth Shopping Centre which has been a feature of the High Street since the 1970s. On the right can be seen Thorpes hardware shop that has been trading since 1947. This is a third generation business set up by the current owner's grandfather, a radio engineer. Thorpes prides itself on offering 'the highest standard of good old fashioned customer service available today'.

A view of the High Street from around 1909. Like a number of views in this book, this is a postcard but not many were sent from Denmark like this one was! On the far left is the United Reform Church that is now the Loch Fyne Restaurant. Next door is another church – the West Avenue Methodists, now the Trinity Church.

The Earl Grey Inn is on the far right of this postcard from around the beginning of the twentieth century. The building next to the public house is having some work done and boards cover the front with numerous advertising posters being displayed.

Now in the twenty-first century, and the same view as the postcard above, showing a number of changes to the buildings on the High Street. The Earl Grey Inn has the more modern name of Barca art bar while next door a Ladbrokes occupies the premises that was having building work in the early 1900s.

Moving further down the High Street from the photographs on the previous page we have two more pubs here – the Blacksmiths Arms on the far right and the Queen Victoria behind the horse and cart. A couple of men walk down the middle of the road where a busy junction with traffic lights is today. This postcard is from around 1900.

High Street, Gosforth.

Today, the two pubs, the Blacksmiths Arms and the Queen Victoria, are still open on the High Street and have retained their original names. The past decade has seen many local public houses close with the downturn suffered by the licensing trade, however the pubs of Gosforth, particularly those along the High Street, have continued to buck the trend and remain open.

The Invasion of Gosforth Pubs

During the First World War a number of measures were introduced by the Government to curb excessive drinking. There was a fear that drunkenness would cause problems to the war effort and production would suffer in munitions works, shipyards and factories. In 1915 the Chancellor of the Exchequer, David Lloyd George, said Britain was 'fighting Germans, Austrians and Drink, and as far as I can see the greatest of those foes is drink.' Pubs had their opening hours changed so they could only stay open between 12 noon and 2.30 pm in the afternoon and between 6.30 pm and 9.30 pm in the evening. Further restrictions could be imposed in cities and industrial areas. A new order imposed on the pubs of Newcastle on 16th May 1915 would see extraordinary scenes in Gosforth. The *Newcastle Journal* reported:

'Gosforth was besieged by thirsty visitors from Newcastle last night. The public houses in the city were, under the new order, closed from 2.30 in the afternoon, but at Gosforth they were open from six o'clock until nine as usual. This was well known in the town, and after six there was a great exodus of people to where a 'drink' was to be had. The tramcars were packed, and in the streets of Gosforth loads of passengers were deposited for nearly two hours.

'The inns in the place were crowded out, and some hundreds of intending customers had to go thirsty away. There was a procession from public house to public house, only to find every bar, taproom and sitting room packed to the utmost capacity.'

Church Road, Gosforth.

The corner of Church Road and the High Street in the early 1900s. The Queen Victoria pub is on the far right. This pub was owned by James Deuchar for a number of years before being taken over by Newcastle Breweries in the mid 1950s. Note the pub's door on the corner later became a window as shown in the photograph below.

Over a hundred years later and the peaceful scene above has been replaced by a set of traffic lights. Railings are needed to separate pedestrians from the cars whereas in the early 1900s it was safe to stand in the road. Fortunately, most of the buildings have retained their distinctive character.

The corner of the High Street and Salters Road today. On the far left is the Gosforth Hotel while opposite is the old Fire Station that served the local community for almost a hundred years before closing in 1990. Further up, on the same side, is the care home that was built on the site of the Royalty Cinema (see page 33).

12

A Busy High Street

Today Gosforth High Street is a busy commercial centre with thriving shops, pubs, restaurants, coffee shops and other businesses. This has been the case for over a hundred years, however, changes in shopping behaviour and fashions have meant some of the businesses along the High Street have long disappeared.

Kelly's trade directory of 1929 lists the following shops on Gosforth High Street:

nine grocers, eight butchers, eight confectioners, six fruiters/greengrocers, five bakers, five chemists, five ladies/children outfitters, four ladies hairdressers, three fishmongers, two milliners, two drapers, two tobacconists and two stationers. At this time there were also seven banks. Other more unusual trades that were listed included a French polisher, dog food dealer and saddler.

The majority of those traders were local family-run concerns although there were some national and international names such as the British & Argentine Meat Co Ltd at number 222 High Street.

One of the shops on the High Street for many years was Broughs, seen here in 1952. This chain of grocers introduced an early form of self-service which had started in American supermarkets. Another of Broughs innovations was an early example of home delivery service. Orders were taken by the shop and deliveries were made to the customer's door by horse-drawn vehicles. This style of mini-supermarket is now a model used by a number of the giant supermarket chains to have a presence on the high street.

Right: An advert for Broughs from 1939 with tea on sale at 2s 4d a pound. At this time, as well as the Gosforth store at 140 High Street (telephone 52123), there were also Broughs branches in New Bridge Street, Westgate Road and Heaton Road.

BROUGHS, Ltd.

for

Finest Quality

GROCERIES

and

PROVISIONS

at Moderate Prices

Try Our GOLDEN BLEND TEA at — 2/4 per lb.

Coals From Gosforth

Right: The Brandling family's Gosforth Colliery in the 1840s. Work began on sinking the shaft in 1825 and coal was first drawn on 31st January 1829. The coal was transported by waggonway the three and a half miles to the Tyne by fixed steam engines.

Sailing ships then carried the coal to various ports with the most important being London. On the London market the coals were known as 'Gosforth Wallsend'. In 1836, 127 ships arrived in the Thames from the Tyne with 44,037 tons of this coal.

The phrase 'Taking Coals to Newcastle' had already been in existence for hundreds years when Gosforth Colliery first opened. Newcastle was the largest coal exporter in the world, in the 1500s it was shipping out 15,000 tons every year, and coals from Gosforth made up only

a fraction of that arriving at the staithes on the Tyne in the nineteenth century. Both banks of the river had vessels loaded up with coals from Northumberland and Durham mines. At one time, keels transported the coal to larger sea-going vessels but the work of the keelmen began to decline when staithes began to load directly into colliers.

Coal from Gosforth Colliery was transported on the already existing waggonway that took the coal from Coxlodge Colleries to Wallsend Staithes. After the colleries closed at the end of the nineteenth century, Tyneside Tramways built a line for their trams on the route of the old Coxlodge Waggonway in the early 1900s. Today a stretch of the old Coxlodge Waggonway has been converted into a cycle path (*left*).

Right: Wallsend Staithes where coals from Gosforth arrived for shipment to London aboard sailing ships in the early nineteenth century.

The executors of Reverend Brandling ran Gosforth Colliery after his death until it was taken over by John Bowes and Partners. One of the partners, Charles Mark Palmer, set about addressing the problem of reducing the cost of transporting coal to markets. Sailing ships could

take weeks for the journey from the Tyne to London. In 1852 Palmer established a shipyard at Jarrow and in the same year they built the *John Bowes* – the first steam screw collier.

The iron-hulled vessel went down the slipway at Jarrow on 27th July 1852. At £10,000 she was not cheap but soon proved a sound investment cutting the trip to London to only days. In the next two years no less than 25 colliers were built at Palmer's yard.

The *John Bowes* was just one of the many colliers that took Gosforth coal to the London markets. These coastal colliers were immortalised at the beginning of the twentieth century by John Masefield in his poem 'Cargoes':

Dirty British coaster with a salt-caked smoke stack,

Butting through the Channel in the mad March days,

With a cargo of Tyne coal

The launch of the *John Bowes* from Palmer's shipyard at Jarrow from *The Illustrated London News*. The *John Bowes* was built with the sailing rig to supplement her steam-driven propeller. After various refits, changes of name and owners she was to have a working life of over eighty years. In October 1933, as the *Villa Selgas* carrying a cargo of iron ore, she was lost in the Bay of Biscay.

Coxlodge Colliery was less than a mile west of the Gosforth mine and was also owned by the Brandling family. It predated Gosforth Colliery and the Jubilee Pit (*left*) which was named in celebration of the Golden Jubilee of George III in 1810.

Right: The Regent Pit at Coxlodge Colliery was named in honour of the Prince Regent who later became George IV. It opened shortly after the Jubilee Pit with coal from both taken along the waggonway to Wallsend.

Left and right: The Regent Centre Business Park now stands on the site of the old colliery and in earlier years a road was named after it.

The Great Race at Gosforth Aerodrome

On 24th July 1911 an estimated crowd of 30,000 to 40,000 spectators gathered at Gosforth Aerodrome to see the arrival of competitors in the Daily Mail Circuit of Britain Air Race. The race for a £10,000 first prize had started from Brooklands in Surrey with planned stopovers in Harrogate and Gosforth before going on to Edinburgh then heading back to the starting point via the west coast.

From 7 o'clock in the morning the flow of traffic on the Great North Road was compared to Newcastle Race Week. Tramcars, motor cars, wagonettes, taxis and cycles took people to the gates where they joined a queue – at times half a mile long – to gain entry. The admission charges were one shilling, reserved enclosure two shillings and special enclosure three shillings.

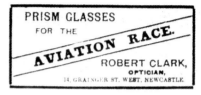

PRISM GLASSES FOR THE AVIATION RACE.
ROBERT CLARK, OPTICIAN, 14, GRAINGER ST. WEST, NEWCASTLE.

A Newcastle optician took advantage of the Air Race to attract business in 1911.

The surviving entrants making the 69-mile journey from Harrogate were advised to follow the North Eastern Railways line from Northallerton, Darlington, Ferryhill then the Leamside track keeping Durham Cathedral on the left then crossing the Wear at Penshaw on to Pelaw crossing the Tyne at Walker before landing at Gosforth.

On route from the Yorkshire spa town one of the most famous flyers, Colonel Samuel Franklin Cody, had a crash. After losing his way while flying over County Durham he decided to land at Brandon Hill to get his bearings but he landed on boggy ground and immediately tried to take off again. His machine failed to take to the air and it hit the top of a stone wall, went through a hedge and came to rest in a field at Pringle House Farm. It appeared that this would put Cody out of the race and the *Sunderland Daily Echo* reported he had retired from the contest and stated the news caused great disappointment at Newcastle, where he is a great favourite. However, the intrepid aviator was determined to make it to Gosforth and an extra incentive to make it was a special prize on offer. The Northumberland and Durham Aero Club and its patron, Sir Charles Parsons, put up a prize of £40 (over £4,000 in today's money) for the first all-British machine to reach Gosforth.

On coming to rest at Brandon, Cody walked to the nearest post office and telegraphed his support team for assistance. With damage to the undercarriage, wings and propeller it did appear that he would have to drop out of the race but help soon arrived. Mechanics from the nearby colliery with the help of Cody's own mechanics, who arrived just after noon, got the aeroplane airworthy. Cody also had local women to thank for spending the whole afternoon sewing the torn canvas of the plane. Cody not only made it to Gosforth to pick up the prize but went on to be one of four men to complete the race.

Colonel Cody leaving Gosforth for Edinburgh in an early form of crash helmet but no parachute. Unlike his main rivals who flew monoplanes, Cody flew a biplane in the race. American-born Cody was a great showmen like his namesake and compatriot Buffalo Bill. He too toured in Wild West Shows before settling in England in the 1890s.

The first man to land at Gosforth was Frenchman Jules Vedrines just ahead of his fellow countryman Naval Lieutenant Jean Louis Conneau. Conneau used the nom de plume Andre Beaumont because he was not permitted to use his real name as he was an officer in the French Navy. James Valentine was the first Englishman to land at Gosforth followed by

Gustav Hamel. Although he left Gosforth first, Vedrines was eventually beaten to the first prize by Conneau who covered the 1,010 mile course in 22 hours 28 minutes 18 seconds at an average speed of 46 miles an hour. James Valentine finished in third place and Cody fourth and last to finish the gruelling course.

Jules Vedrines, the first man to arrive at Gosforth.

Jean Louis Conneau (aka Andre Beaumont) who won the Daily Mail Air Race in 1911.

AEROPLANE RACE. GOSFORTH PARK JULY 24TH 1911 R.G.

Above and right: Two postcard views showing the large crowd that gathered around James Valentine's plane that landed at Gosforth Park on 24th July 1911 during the Daily Mail Circuit of Britain Air Race. Valentine was the first English pilot to arrive at Gosforth that day and eventually finished third in the race.

AEROPLANE RACE J. VALENTINE AT GOSFORTH PARK JULY 24TH 1911 R.G.

One of the competitors who had to retire from the race with engine trouble before reaching Gosforth was Bentfield 'Benny' Charles Hucks who made a return visit to Tyneside two years later. In February 1913 he spent a week at Gosforth engaged in flying for a local firm. He was hired as part of a goods despatch experiment for the Robert Sinclair Tobacco Company of Newcastle. Hucks' Bleriot monoplane made exhibition flights as well as making deliveries of a new brand of tobacco to outlying towns and villages. One of these was to Seaham Harbour on 11th February. After a delay caused by ground mist he took off and landed at Seaham 17 minutes later at 3.30 pm. After delivering his goods and taking on fuel he returned to Gosforth in time for tea.

The following year on the outbreak of war Benny Hucks joined the Royal Flying Corps. As an experienced flyer he was sent to the Western Front but was sent home with pleurisy. He then worked as a test pilot at Hendon but only four days before the end of the war he died of double pneumonia following Spanish Flu.

Benny Hucks in the aeroplane he flew at Gosforth in 1913 to make deliveries for Robert Sinclair Tobacco Company.

Right: Bentfield Hucks in his Bleriot monoplane from a postcard produced by Robert Sinclair Tobacco to promote flights and exhibition at Gosforth in 1913.

FLYING.

TO-DAY (Saturday)

Mr B. C. HUCKS

WILL MAKE A

Flight Down the River Tyne

FROM

Scotswood to Tynemouth

AND

Back to the Aerodrome at Gosforth Park,

LEAVING ABOUT 12.

A SPECIAL EXHIBITION

will be given at

Gosforth Park Aerodrome

From 3 p.m. until Dusk (Weather Permitting).

ROBERT SINCLAIR

Tobacco Co., Ltd.

Flying at Gosforth.

MR. B. C. HUCKS will give an EXHIBITION OF FLYING **TO-DAY, and each day till** further notice, at the GOSFORTH PARK AERODROME, at 11.30, whether he makes the CROSS-COUNTRY FLIGHT FOR THE ROBERT SINCLAIR TOBACCO CO., or not.

LATEST PARTICULARS AT

61, GRAINGER STREET WEST.

Left: Two adverts from the *Newcastle Journal* for Bentfield Hucks' appearances at the Aerodrome at Gosforth in February 1913. Hucks also made a flight down the River Tyne from Scotswood to Tynemouth, followed by a special exhibition at the Aerodrome.

In August 1913 another of the stalwarts of the 1911 Air Race lost his life. Colonel Cody was on a test flight over Farnborough with a passenger, cricketer William Evans, when the aviator's latest plane, the Cody Floatplane, broke-up in mid-air and crashed to the ground killing both men.

If further evidence of the dangers faced by the early aviators was needed it came with the deaths of another three competitors who had appeared at Gosforth in 1911. Gustav Hamel disappeared over the English Channel in his monoplane in May 1914. James Valentine died as a result of wounds flying with the Royal Flying Corps in Russia during the First World War. Jules Vedrines was killed in 1919 when his plane crashed on a flight to Rome.

Hospitals in Gosforth

Right: A postcard sent from the W.J. Sanderson Orthopaedic Hospital for Children in 1938 informing the parents of Rosa that she had underwent an operation and her parents could visit on Saturday.

FROM THE MATRON.

The W. J. Sanderson Orthopædic Hospital School for Children, North Avenue, Gosforth, Newcastle-upon-Tyne 3.

2.9.38.

Rosa underwent an operation yesterday. Her progress has been satisfactory and parents will be permitted to visit her on Saturday first between 2 and 4 p.m.

W.J. Sanderson was a philanthropist and former Lord Mayor of Newcastle who in the late 19th century set up a home for crippled children in Whickham. When this proved to be too small, a home in Gosforth was opened in 1897 at a cost of £10,000. Originally called the 'Home for Destitute Crippled Children', its aim was originally to treat those who could not be housed in the workhouse. The building was enlarged in 1914 to house up to 125 children. In the 1930s it was designated an Orthopaedic Hospital. Before the days of the NHS and when diseases such as polio were common in this country, institutions such as these were vital for the care of the sick and disabled. The hospital eventually became part of the National Health Service and was still treating children and adults in the 1970s.

NORTHERN COUNTIES CRIPPLES HOME, GOSFORTH.

Left: A postcard of the hospital with some young lads and a gardener posing for the photographer.

Right: A postcard titled 'Northumberland War Hospital, Gosforth'. This hospital was originally built to house mentally ill patients in 1869 at a cost of £65,000. Over the years the building was extended and in 1911 the population of Gosforth was stated as being '15,490, including 892 inmates and 164 officials and their families in Newcastle City Mental Hospital'. This postcard dates from the First World War when the hospital was taken over for wounded soldiers. It was handed back in 1921 and after the founding of the NHS was renamed St Nicholas Hospital. The hospital is still used today and offers a range of mental health services.

Northumberland War Hospital, Gosforth.

Gosforth Park Racecourse and the Northumberland Plate

The Northumberland Plate is one of the most famous handicaps in the horseracing calendar. Known locally as the 'Pitmen's Derby' the Plate was first run in 1833 on the Town Moor. Two members of the Town Moor Grandstand Committee bought the 807 acre Gosforth Park Estate for £60,500 and soon the race was switched to a new course constructed there. Stands and stabling were built and completed in time for the first running of the Plate at Gosforth Park in 1882.

A postcard of the Grandstand on the Town Moor.

The Tinman Takes The Plate

The year after the inaugural running of the Northumberland Plate at Gosforth saw a great horse and even greater jockey claim the race. Fred Archer was one of the sporting giants of the Victorian Age. He is seen on the left keeping warm before a race. The thirteen-time champion jockey won no less than 21 Classics, including the Epsom Derby on four occasions.

At 5ft 10ins tall, his frame was to cause him weight problems throughout his career in the saddle. His nickname The Tinman came from the nineteenth century slang for money – tin. He certainly made a fortune from racing and as he was a big gambler a lot of it slipped through his hands.

The prize money for the Northumberland Plate in 1883 was large enough to bring the greatest jockey in the country to Tyneside. His mount that day was Barcaldine which had won all 11 of its previous races. There was no danger of the five year old horse losing its unbeaten record with Archer on board. Barcaldine romped home by two lengths in a canter.

To make his riding weight of 8st 6lbs he followed a near-starvation diet combined with Turkish baths and daily purgatives known as 'Archer's Mixture'.

Tragedy struck his private life when his first son died after only a few hours then his wife died giving birth to their second child. The loss of his wife at the age of only 23 sent the jockey into a deep depression. On the afternoon of 8th November 1886 he committed suicide by putting a revolver in his mouth and pulling the trigger. He was only 29 years old and the whole nation mourned the loss of the greatest jockey of the day.

He had rode 2,748 winners from just over 8,000 mounts – he was first past the winning post once every three starts.

The tall figure of Fred Archer in the saddle. Lester Piggott, champion jockey in the last century, had a similar build and was known as 'The Long Fellow'.

Horse-drawn trams and carriages in Gosforth on race day in the 1890s. At this time the Plate was run on a Wednesday just like Epsom Derby. The running of the big race was changed to a Saturday in the 1950s allowing many more workers to attend. Eventually the Derby followed suit and is also now run on a weekend.

Gosforth Park early in the last century. After the estate was bought in the early 1880s a Grandstand was built on the side of Gosforth House. The part of the house seen on the left of the picture was converted into a public house – the Gosforth Park Hotel. This famous watering hole for punters is still going strong today and is now known as the Border Minstrel.

Above: A postcard view of the Grandstand built on the side of Gosforth House. On the right a group of ladies with a young boy are taking a stroll. Are they the nannies mentioned on page 6?

Right: A picturesque scene of Gosforth Park with the Grandstand in the background.

The weighing room and the entrance for owners and trainers in the converted buildings of Gosforth House. In recent years £11 million has been spent on improving facilities for spectators. These have included new stands and parade ring.

Two postcard views of the Paddock at Gosforth Park in the early days.

The Head Waiter and the Jockey Knight

When racing was suspended at Gosforth during the Second World War the Grandstand and other buildings were taken over by the Army. When the war ended the racecourse was still not ready to stage the 1946 Plate. The race was switched to Aintree and was won by Gusty ridden by Harry Wragg.

Harry 'The Head Waiter' Wragg towering over Gordon Richards. Wragg's solitary victory in the Northumberland Plate came on Merseyside not Tyneside.

Friseur just gets to the winning post first to give Gordon Richards his only Northumberland Plate success in 1954. Like Fred Archer before him Richards dominated the racing scene, being champion jockey on 26 occasions and became the first jockey knighted for his services to the sport. He had to wait until the twilight of his career before winning the big two Derbies – the Epsom on Pinza in 1953 and the Pitmen's the following year.

The Queen Mother at Gosforth on Northumberland Plate Day in 1962. She is chatting with Geoff Littlewood who rode the winner Bordone.

A long walk back for 'The Long Fellow'. Lester Piggott had been unseated by Sunny Way in the 1961 Northumberland Plate. Six years before he had claimed his one and only Plate victory aboard Little Cloud.

The Northumberland Plate is as popular as ever and drew huge crowds on 25th June 2016. A thrilling race was won by Antiquarium for a prize of over £86,000. Jockey James McDonald piloted the winner home to the delight of punters in the packed stands.

Below: The entrance gates to Gosforth Park Racecourse in 2014. As well as horse racing, the venue also hosts, conferences, exhibitions, weddings, antique and craft fairs and many other events.

Gosforth at War and Peace

Gosforth War Memorial

A postcard of the people who took part in a fancy dress parade held on 9th November 1918 to raise money for the Gosforth & Coxlodge War Memorial Fund. Several are holding collecting tins with 'War Memorial Fund' on them. The day before the following article appeared in the *Newcastle Journal*:

'Good progress is being made with respect to the Gosforth War Memorial, and, in order to assist the funds, a fancy dress parade has been fixed for tomorrow. The event will occupy the greater part of the day, for the whole of the urban district to be paraded. A start will be made from the Coxlodge Social Club at 10 o'clock to 12; Salter's Road 1; High Street, 1 to 2; Elmfield Road and Northumberland Avenue, 2 to 3; Ashburton and district, 3 to 4; Rectory Terrace and district, 4.30; South Gosforth, 5; and concluding at the Globe Picture House at 6 o'clock. The Coxlodge Silver Band, specially augmented for the day, will head the parade, which will include several humorous and fancy costumes, representing *Old Bill of the Better 'Ole*, Charlie Chaplin, pierrots, bakers, land girls, nurses, Red Riding Hood, Bo-Peep and the Kaiser. There will be at least 40 members of the parade, and en route collectors will be busy taking up subscriptions.'

The Better 'Ole was a music comedy first performed in London in 1917. The main character, Old Bill a British soldier who has a series of adventures during the First World War, was created by cartoonist Captain Bruce Bairnsfather (1887-1959). Born into a military family in British India (now Pakistan), Bairnsfather failed his exams to Sandhurst and joined the Cheshire Regiment. He resigned in 1907 to become an artist but at the start of the First World War he enlisted in the Royal Warwickshire Regiment. When hospitalised with shell shock and hearing damage, he developed his humorous series of cartoons featuring life during the war (*right*). His most famous character was 'Old Bill', an elderly soldier with a walrus moustache who became very popular on comic postcards and in books and magazines such as *The Bystander*.

Two weeks after the 1918 Gosforth fancy dress parade, a meeting was held in the United Methodist Schoolroom, to discuss what form the proposed war memorial would take. Mr G.E. Brown, Chairman of the Gosforth Urban District Council, presided over the meeting where a vote was taken which decided the money raised would go towards building a welfare centre.

"Well, if you knows of a better 'ole, go to it."

The Gosforth Memorial Welfare Centre on Church Road. The foundation stone was laid on 12th March 1924 and it was opened the following January. An inscription by the main door reads: 'This building was erected by public subscription as a memorial to the local men who fell in the Great War 1914-1918.'

A War Memorial Pillar was erected in front of the Welfare Clinic which was later moved to Gosforth Central Park.

Northumberland War Hospital

Right: A postcard view of Northumberland War Hospital, Gosforth. The *Morpeth Herald* of 27th October 1916 gave this account of a presentation to the hospital:

'A most suitable gift for the Northumberland War Hospital, Gosforth, an open pavilion with accommodation for 36 beds, was made to the institution on Saturday by the Elswick and Scotswood War Workers Fund. The presentation was performed in the presence

of a large company most of whom by their weekly contributions had made the fund such a success.

'Having a south aspect, the pavilion is pleasingly decorated in green and white, and is lighted and heated by electricity.

'Mr George Young presided over the proceedings, and the pavilion was formally handed over to Colonel G.G. Adams, AMS, for the hospital authorities by Mr J.J. Berry, the secretary of the fund.

'Mr Berry, in his remarks, made some interesting references to the Elswick and Scotswood War Workers' Fund which was begun on the initiation of Madame Beatrice Bartlett. At first the income of the fund was £80 a month but now it was £1,100. The total amount disbursed, including donations to the Prince of Wales' Fund and the Lord Mayor's Fund, was approximately £50,000. In addition to providing articles for almost all the Allied countries, six million cigarettes and 15,000 books for our soldiers and sailors, the fund had furnished a motor ambulance for the front at a cost of £750, an open-air pavilion similar to the one round which they were gathered to the Armstrong College, and an X-rays apparatus for use in Gosforth War Hospital. The cost of the pavilion was £500, and Mr Berry mentioned that when it was no longer required by the war hospital it would revert back to the fund, in order that it might be handed over to the Royal Victoria Infirmary, the Barrasford Sanatorium, or some similar institution.

'Colonel Adams expressed his thanks and his appreciation for the gift, and after votes of thanks moved by Mr F.B. Gibbs and Mr J. Gibbon the National Anthem was sung.'

Babies' Helmets

Two weeks after the Second World War was declared in September 1939, Gosforth Urban District Council issued the following instructions:

'The distribution of babies' helmets to residents in the Gosforth Urban District will take place on Sunday and Monday, the 17th and 18th September between 10 am and 1 pm and 2 pm and 6 pm, at the Maternity Child Welfare Centre, Church Road, Gosforth.

'Mothers or other persons in charge of babies should bring their babies with them.

'These babies' helmets in the first instance will be given to residents of Gosforth who were registered and all others who have not registered should do so at once. The helmets must not be taken outside the district, and will not be given to residents of Gosforth who have temporarily left the district.'

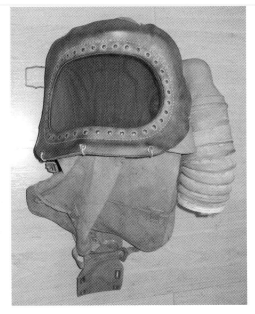

Right: A babies' helmet issued at the beginning of the war when it was feared Germany would drop gas on to the population. Thankfully, the helmet and other respirators were not needed as gas was never used during the Second World War.

Collecting Scrap Metal

Workmen removing tram tracks from Station Road at South Gosforth in September 1940. That month Herbert Morrison, Minister for Supply, had appealed to local councils to collect more scrap metal for the war effort. Old, unused tram lines were just some of the items that were scrapped, however, much of the metal collected during the Second World War was unsuitable to be recycled.

In 2017 a bus stop now stands in front of the shops on Station Road.

Fund Raising

The people of Gosforth took part in a number of fund-raising efforts during the Second World War. Special events, often lasting a week, were held such as the Newcastle & Gosforth Merchant Navy Week in 1944. The illustration on the right shows that the target for this particular appeal was £25,000. During the week in June there were dances, concerts, physical training displays and even challenge cricket matches to raise money towards the target.

Other campaigns that Gosforth took part in during the war included the Tyneside War Weapons Week, Warship Week and the Spitfire Fund. In 1940 the Tyneside War Weapons Week set a target to raise £3million. Local people were encouraged to buy National Savings Certificates, War Bonds, Defence Bonds or make deposits into the Post Office or Trustees Savings Banks. An advert at the time listed what the money could buy: bullet – 6d; grenade – 4 shillings, pistol – £4; rifle – £6; machine gun – £100; tank – £15,000. After the war you could withdraw your money with interest.

Home Guard

Right: An advert from the *Evening Chronicle* appealing for men to come forward to be despatch riders for the LDV – the Local Defence Volunteers –

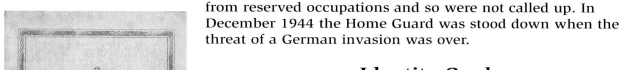

for the Gosforth area. Formed in May 1940, the LDV was later renamed the Home Guard by Winston Churchill. Most members were men too old for the regular forces or were workers from reserved occupations and so were not called up. In December 1944 the Home Guard was stood down when the threat of a German invasion was over.

Identity Cards

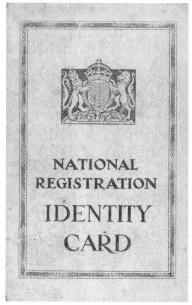

In March 1943 eight people were fined after police checked for Identity Cards at Gosforth Greyhound Racing Stadium. Nearly 5,000 people who were at the Stadium on Saturday, 30th January were asked for their cards and a large number did not have them. Those not carrying the document were given two days to show them at a police station. Eight people failed to do so and were each fined £2 at Moot Hall Police Court.

Identity Cards (*left*), introduced following the National Registration Act of 1939, had to be carried at all time and it was a criminal offence not to produce one when challenged by a police officer. It was not until 1952, seven years after the war ended, that they were scrapped.

Careless Talk Costs Lives

A postcard of 'Little Bridge, Gosforth'. The card was sent to Bradford in 1943 but the image is much earlier, probably before the First World War. Perhaps with the shortage of paper during the Second World War, and few postcards being produced, the sender of this card used an old one from their collection. Who sent the card is a mystery and says he is 'Somewhere in England'. People were told not to say too much during wartime in case valuable information got into the wrong hands. The saying was: 'Careless talk costs lives.'

Public Houses

On 6th and 7th October 1852 the sale of the estates of the Brandling family of Gosforth was held in the long-room of the Queen's Head in Newcastle. No less than four public houses were included in the sale. Details of the auction were recorded in *Remarkable Events, Connected with the Borough of Gateshead*. The London firm of Farebrother, Clark and Lye conducted proceedings before a 'large assemblage of capitalists of the town and district'.

On the first day of the sale the Freehold public house Duke of Wellington, Coxlodge with Land was withdrawn at £810 and another Freehold public house Shoulder of Mutton, Coxlodge with Land was also not sold.

There was better luck on Day Two of the sale when the Bay Horse public house, Haddricks Mill with Ground, Quarry, Cottages etc was bought by Philip Smith of Gateshead for £1,180. The Freehold public house Ship and Land, Longbenton was sold to Mr Swan, a solicitor, for £1,100.

The very first lot of the sale was Gosforth Hall and Farm which went for £25,200. Part of the old hall was later converted into a public house. Today this is known as the Border Minstrel and a meeting place for thirsty racegoers.

The Border Minstrel public house in 1961. The Gosforth Park Hotel was renamed Border Minstrel after the Northumberland Plate winner of 1927.

At the 1852 auction the Shoulder of Mutton was described as consisting of four ground floor rooms, five first floor rooms, bar, cellar with stable and good garden. Despite these selling points it remained unsold and by the 1870s the licence was transferred to a pub built on the corner of Salters Road and the High Street – The Gosforth Hotel.

Left: The Gosforth Hotel today with its pre-First World War glazed tiled frontage.

The Duke of Wellington was another pub that did not meet the reserve price at the 1852 auction. The present day pub bearing that name is a 1930s rebuild of an old inn. This pub was built on a much grander scale with an upstairs lounge that could cater for 240 who were entertained by a resident orchestra. The Iron Duke was also well represented in the decor of the pub with personal letters and pictures of the Battle of Waterloo adorning the walls.

The Duke of Wellington, Kenton Lane, in the 1930s.

The Queen Victoria on the corner of Church Road and the High Street. After periods as the Northern Lights and Ye Olde Jockey the pub returned to its original name for life in the twenty-first century.

Right: The Barca art bar on the High Street in 2017. This nineteenth century beerhouse was formerly the Earl Grey Inn (seen below before the Second World War). When Vaux took it over in the 1930s they acquired a full licence allowing spirits to be served.

Just along from the Queen Victoria, on the High Street, is the former beerhouse the Blacksmiths Arms. Like a number of modern pubs, it has moved with the times and hosts live music nights.

As well as having a wide selection of drinks behind the bar, the Brandling Arms on the High Street also serves everything from homemade burgers to sausage and mash and from fish and chips to Sunday roasts.

Building Recycling – Wetherspoon pub, the Job Bulman, is housed in the former post office on St Nicholas Avenue. Job Bulman gave his to name to Bulman Village which later became part of today's Gosforth.

Another High Street pub is the County where customers can sit at the tables outside while drinking real ale and watching life go by. The pub famously had to open its Gentlemen Only Buffet to ladies after the introduction of the Sex Discrimination Act in 1975.

The Three Mile Inn, seen here in the 1970s, was built on the Great North Road in the 1930s when new pubs were going up on the outskirts of towns and cities to cater for the ever expanding suburbs.

The Three Mile Inn's Alpine Room in 1970 designed in the style of a Swiss chalet. At this time there was also the Regency Room with an *a la carte* menu, Red Room Bar and Blue Room which held wedding receptions and meetings. The pub was refurbished again at the turn of this century.

The Falcon's Nest is a farmhouse style pub restaurant on Rotary Way and is handy for drinkers and diners from the four nearby golf courses as well as Gosforth Park Racecourse.

Left: When the Royal George opened at Brunton Park in the 1960s it had a lounge and buffet but surprisingly no bar. Built in the Dutch-style with pantiled roof, in contrast to a number of Gosforth pubs still going strong after more than 150 years, the Royal George's life span was barely half a century. The Royal George closed in 2008 and despite efforts to save the pub it was demolished and a care home built on the site.

On Kenton Road, the Coxlodge, dating from the 1860s, did not have a full licence until just before the end of the nineteenth century. It was known to locals as the 'Trap' right up to its closure.

Opened in 1958, the Jubilee is seen here in 2014. This popular pub on Jubilee Road was closed for several months at the beginning of 2017 following a fire.

The Millstone on Haddricks Mill Road. The present building dates from around 1900 when local brewer J.H. Graham rebuilt the original pub. In the last century the Millstone's owners have included Wearside-based James Deuchar, local company Newcastle Hotels and the nationwide Bass Breweries.

The Victory on Killingworth Road in the last century. The pub is still going strong in 2017, alongside its two near neighbours in South Gosforth.

Right: The Brandling Villa on Haddricks Mill Road in 1968. One of the events the pub has staged has been a Sausage and Beer Festival. Over 600 lbs of sausage was consumed before thirsts were quenched with gallons of ale.

Cinemas

The Globe

The Globe on Salters Road opened on 19th December 1910 in the age of silent pictures. In these early years of the cinema the theatre still had vaudeville acts entertaining their patrons at Gosforth twice each evening and Saturday afternoons. For screenings of the films with no sound the Globe Orchestra interpreted the action.

In 1935 the then owners British-Gaumont sold off the Globe to E.J. Hinge who was already co-owner of the Royalty situated less than a hundred yards along Gosforth High Street. The Globe was part of the Hinge's Circuit of cinemas which also included the Rialto at Benwell, Ritz at Forest Hall and Regal at Two Ball Lonnen, Fenham.

The decline in going to the pictures is attributed to the rise of television in the 1950s. On Tyneside a crucial date was the introduction of Tyne-Tees Television's Channel 8 at the end of the decade. Between 1958 and 1963 no less than two dozen Newcastle cinemas closed and one of these was the Globe.

The comedy *No, My Darling Daughter* was the last film to be shown at the Globe on 25th November 1961. Like many cinemas that closed at this time the Globe became a bingo hall. The old theatre building is still in use today housing a Chinese restaurant, a beauty salon and an interiors company.

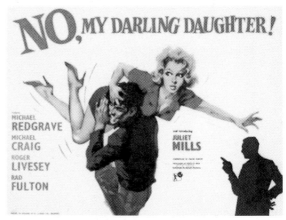

A screening of the *Black Widow* starring Sunderland-born Christine Norden at the Globe in May 1954. Later in the week the romantic comedy *Roman Holiday* with Audrey Hepburn and Gregory Peck was shown.

The end of an era at the Globe – the last picture show.

Left: A postcard of Salters Road. On the far right is a lady on her hands and knees cleaning the steps of the Globe.

The former Globe Cinema on Salters Road in 2017. Over a century after opening as Gosforth's first picture house the building now houses the Gosforth Palace Chinese Restaurant, S.O. Beautiful Boutique Beauty Salon and Gosforth Interiors.

The Royalty

When the Royalty opened on Gosforth High Street on 17th October 1934 it was at the dawn of the age of the talkies. The new building housing Gosforth's second cinema was an impressive structure.

The dazzling white finish to the exterior was created with a special Snowcrete mixture and once the dome was floodlit with green, blue, yellow and scarlet neon lights it made an imposing sight.

The interior of the new cinema was no less impressive with one local reporter declaring: 'I have never been in a more attractive and more comfortable Northern picture-hall outside Newcastle. The sound reproduction is as good as I have heard anywhere in the country and I know of only one other cinema in Newcastle or on Tyneside that can boast such perfect lighting scheme.'

The general manager, Robert Gilbertson, had a staff of more than two dozen working under him. These included three projectionists, a dozen usherettes, three cashiers as well as daymen, cleaners, page boys and chocolate boy.

ROYALTY, GOSFORTH
TELEPHONE 52324.
GRAND OPENING
WEDNESDAY, OCT. 17th, at 7.30 p.m.,
By Councillor W. H. BLENKINSOP
(Chairman)
AND MEMBERS OF GOSFORTH U.D.C.
ON THE AIR.
With ROY FOX AND HIS BAND.
Also full supporting programme will be shown.
Whole of Proceeds Devoted to Charities.

THURS. and FRIDAY, Cont. from 6.30 p.m.
Sat., Mat at 2.30 p.m.; Twice Nightly, 6.30-8.45 p.m.
THE GREAT MUSICAL COMEDY—
WONDER BAR.
Box Office Open 11 a.m. to 1 p.m. & 5 p.m. onwards.

The Royalty opened with a performance of *On the Air* with the proceeds going to local charities.

THURSDAY and FRIDAY—Continuous from 6.30 p.m.
SATURDAY—Twice Nightly at 6.30 and 8.45. Matinee at 2.30.
. THE GREAT MUSICAL COMEDY .
WONDER BAR
Starring—AL JOLSON, KAY FRANCIS, DOLORES DEL RIO,
and a huge cast of Stars.

PRICES :	CIRCLE	STALLS		PIT
	1/-	9d		7d
	Reserved 1/3	Reserved 1/-		
	CHILDREN :	6d	5d	4d
FREE CAR PARK.			NO LIGHTS REQUIRED.	

The latest Al Jolson musical *Wonder Bar* was the first film shown at the Royalty after the grand charity opening. Admission prices ranged from 4d for children to Reserved Circle at 1s 3d.

Left: The Royalty not only provided its patrons with the best films but was also a famous Gosforth landmark for half a century.

With audience figures falling, efforts were made to convert the theatre to a bingo hall were prevented by local residents and pop concerts were even tried. The last films screened was the Disney double bill *The Incredible Journey* and *Dumbo* on 30th December 1981.

Right: No mistaking the gleaming white Royalty on the High Street. The building is now gone and replaced by a care home.

Transport

A steam roller owned by Gosforth road contractor William Bland & Son. Mr Bland is listed in the Ward's Trade Directory of 1903-04 as living at Woodbine Terrace. The name of the engine was 'Dora' and it with its workers are featured on a number of old postcards of the area.

More steam power with a train arriving at Kenton Station shortly after opening in 1905. The station was later renamed Kenton Bank and was in use for passengers until 1929. It was used for goods until 1966 and demolished in the early 1970s. The railway line was later used for the Metro, and Kenton Bank Foot Station was built nearby.

Another station that was opened in 1905, and on the same line, was West Gosforth. This station had a similar life to Kenton Bank above – closed for passengers in the 1920s, closed completely in the 1960s and demolished a decade later. The Regent Centre Metro Station occupies part of the old West Gosforth site.

Above: The aftermath of a collision involving two tram cars on the Great North Road in the 1940s. The conductor on the left surveys the damage while the crash has attracted plenty of local onlookers.

Below: No 276, shown here after the smash, was the car that was hit by the tram above.

A Gosforth & Central Station tram car in much better condition than the ones above and left. This popular form of transport survived in Newcastle until 1950.

Another form of transport remembered with fondness is the trolleybus. This yellow-liveried vehicle is off to Gosforth Park. The trolleybus system operated in Newcastle for thirty years from the mid 1930s.

Above: A horse and carriage outside the back of Fred Gees' premises in High Street, Gosforth. This was a time of transition for businesses like Gees as horse-drawn transport such as laundaus, broughams and dog carts were making way for motor vehicles.

Left: Fred Gees' horse-drawn hearse in the last century. In a reversal of the trend towards motorised vehicles in recent years the horse-drawn hearse has made a comeback in funeral corteges.

Left: Another local firm on Gosforth High Street was Robson & Porteous – Bakers & Confectioners at number 166. Here is their delivery van from the late 1950s.

The latest MG Magnette on the forecourt of Gosforth Motor Company in 1960. In the early 1960s, Gosforth Motors were selling the basic Mini at £447 12s 11d (£89 12s 11d deposit and weekly payments of £2 16s 2d) and the Austin Westminster at £1,051 16s 3d.

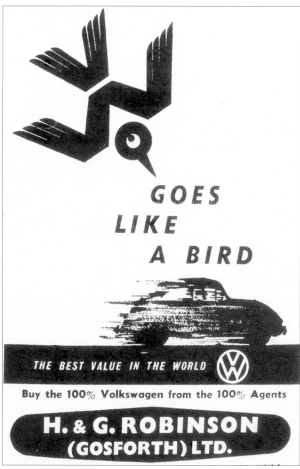

The ageless Volkswagen Beetle advertised at Robinson's Grandstand Garage in 1960.

An advert for Gosforth Motor Co from 1965: *Howay To Gosforth – For your next car!'*

Sporting Life

Rugby Union

Formed in 1877, from its earliest days Gosforth Rugby Union Club played in the famous green and white hoops. In the 1990s after the introduction of professionalism to rugby the club split in two with the professional Newcastle and amateur Gosforth.

One of the legendary players who wore the Gosforth shirt was Roger Uttley (*right*) who played for England on 23 occasions and was part of the British Lions that won the series in South Africa.

Cycling

Gosforth Road Club was formed in 1951 with members wearing green and orange kit. The original meeting place for club runs was the Globe picture house in Salters Road. The club has 180 members who compete in everything from road racing to cyclo-cross and mountain biking to time trialling.

The club's most famous member is Joe Waugh (*right*) the Commonwealth Games gold medallist and two times Olympian. Joe later joined the long-established M. Steel Cycles in South Gosforth.

Tennis Courts

Mixed doubles games at Gosforth Garden Village Tennis Club in the summer of 2014. Based at Rosewood Avenue the club was formed in 1928.

The tennis courts at Gosforth Central Park date from 1932.

Athletics

Gosforth Harriers and Athletic Club was founded in 1927. The club's first General Meeting was held that year in the Queen Victoria public house. A total of 21 club rules were decided upon at this meeting. These included: that the colours would be helio vest and white knickers with a badge on the vest; annual subscriptions for membership would be 2s 6d and for youths 1s 6d and 'That the captain appoints pacemakers and whips on each club night and those members must obey the instructions of the whip and on no account attempt to pass the pacemaker.'

Today the club train around Gosforth Park and surrounding countryside.

Gosforth Greyhound Stadium

Right: An advert for the final of the 1968 Gosforth Cup. The race was won by Hi-Ho Silver with the owner picking up £200 prize money as well as the trophy. A new restaurant extension at the stadium had just opened. Over the years a number of sports were staged at the stadium (*below*) and in 1929 Speedway was introduced but this proved a short-lived venture. Gosforth Stadium finally closed in the 1980s and a supermarket was built on the site.

Asda now stands on the site of the stadium.

South Northumberland Cricket Club

In 2014 South Northumberland Cricket Club celebrated their 150th anniversary. Since being formed in 1864 as Bulman's Village Cricket Club it has become an important part of community life.

Between 1866 and 1882 there was a name change to Gosforth Cricket Club but for most of its long history it has been known under its present title. The 1st XI play in the North East Premier League which they have won ten times. In 2016 the ECB National Club Cricket Championship was won for the third time after beating Swardeston at Northampton's County Ground.

The club have a number of other teams including Under 15s, Under 13s and Under 11s and with 240 boy and girl members the future of the club appears to be in safe hands for the next 150 years.

The pavilion in 2014 as preparations are being made for Junior matches.

The cricket field and the impressive indoor facilities at the Gosforth ground. Opened in 2003 at a cost of £1.5 million, the indoor centre provides year round coaching.

Pigeon Racing

For many years members of Gosforth Homing Society have had their crees at Hollywood Avenue. In 1926 Allen Brothers of Gosforth won the prestigious Up North Combine Melun Race. By the mid 1950s Gosforth, along with its neighbour Coxlodge, were two of 13 Newcastle clubs in the Up North Combine. At this time the Boustead Brothers and Hall & Son were leading members of the club and the Halls came second in the 1954 Bourges Race. The pick up point for the transport of birds to liberation destinations was South Gosforth Railway Station. Baskets of birds were loaded on trains for release points in the south of England and the Continent. The *Evening Chronicle* awarded special prizes in the Brussels 'Chronicle' Cup Race of 1955. As well as sponsoring the Brussels event the local newspaper also sponsored the Lille and Welwyn Garden City races in the 1950s.

Right: Billy Doniger, a veteran of 30 years of racing pigeons, in front of his cree at Hollywood Avenue.

Brian Howie's birds at Hollywood Avenue.

Keith Welling, another member of Gosforth Homing Society.

Gosforth Boys to Premier Footballers

Gosforth's most famous sporting son has to be Alan Shearer. Born in Gosforth on 13th August 1970 and after attending Gosforth High School he went on to become one of England's greatest footballers. He signed for his hometown club for a world record £15million transfer fee and scored 206 goals in 404 League and Cup appearances for Newcastle United. Alan also found the net 30 times in 63 appearances for England.

Robbie Elliott was another local boy who went on to become a professional footballer after attending Gosforth High. Born in Gosforth on Christmas Day 1973 he made his name at Newcastle United before moving to Bolton Wanderers for £2.5million. After spells with Sunderland, Leeds United and Hartlepool United, Robbie later worked for the US Soccer Federation.

Yet another Premier League player who had close ties with Gosforth was Michael Chopra. He was a pupil of Gosforth West Middle School before going on to carve out a football career at Newcastle United. Like Robbie Elliott, he too played for United's biggest rivals. He joined Sunderland from Cardiff City in 2007 for £5million before returning to the Welsh club.

Golf Clubs

Right: An aerial view from the 1960s showing Northumberland Golf Club. Formed in 1898, the course was constructed in and around Gosforth Park Racecourse. The Club House can be seen at the bottom of the photograph.

There are three more golf clubs in the area. The City of Newcastle Golf Club was formed in 1891 on the Town Moor then moved to Three Mile Bridge sixteen years later. Gosforth Golf Club opened in 1906 and seven years later its Club House was a target of a Suffragette bomb (see page 42). A more recent addition is Parklands Golf Club (formerly Wideopen GC) that was opened in 1971.

Bowling Greens

Above and below: Players enjoying a Sunday morning game at Gosforth Empire Bowling Club. The club dates from the 1970s but the oldest bowling club in Gosforth was established in 1897 as part of the Gosforth Recreation Company. The green at West Park was ready for play in 1902.

Gosforth Garden Village Bowls Club at Rosewood Avenue.

The bowling green at Gosforth Central Park which opened in 1934.

41

Suffragettes Attack the Globe and Gosforth Golf Club

Gosforth and Coxlodge Liberal Association booked the Globe Theatre for a meeting on Saturday afternoon, 22nd February 1913. Their guest speaker was Alexander Ure MP, the Lord Advocate for Scotland. The following Monday the *Newcastle Journal* reported: 'Suffragists had been busy before the meeting and earlier in the day a plate-glass window of the theatre had been smashed with a hammer, which was found inside. Attached to it was a label with the words, *Let fresh air into politics by votes from women.'* There were also Suffragettes in the audience when Ure was speaking and when two of them interrupted him they were ejected.

This was one of the most militant periods in the fight for Votes for Women. The leader of the Women's Social and Political Union, Emmeline Pankhurst, had been arrested in London a few days before the Globe incident. She was charged with incitement in connection with the bombing of the residence of the Chancellor of the Exchequer, Lloyd George. Her arrest, trial and sentence to three years imprisonment sent the Suffragettes on a campaign of action – placing firebombs in letter boxes, breaking shop windows and damaging property. Sport venues and sporting events around the country were also targeted. Golf clubs, bowling greens, racecourses and tennis clubs were attacked. On 26th February 1913 a woman was arrested on the All England tennis courts at Wimbledon carrying firelighters, oil, shavings and a trowel. During the Epsom Derby on 4th June 1913 Emily Davison, whose family came from Morpeth and Longhorsley, stepped in front of the King's horse during the race. She died of her injuries four days later and the Women's Social and Political Union conferred her as a martyr to the cause.

The funeral of Emily Davison at Morpeth.

A month after Emily Davison's death and the day after Sylvia Pankhurst was arrested for inciting violence in a speech she made in Trafalgar Square the activists' campaign returned to Gosforth. On the morning of 8th July 1913 an attempt was made to blow up the pavilion of Gosforth Golf Club. When Police Sergeant Davidson was doing his rounds he discovered the bomb near the building. The only reason the device had not gone off was because the long fuse had burnt out before setting off the charge.

Right: Within weeks of the Club House at Gosforth Golf Club being completed in 1913 the new pavilion almost fell victim to a Suffragette bomb. The start of the First World War was to see an end to the militant campaign. When Emmeline Pankhurst was released from prison she worked for the war effort by encouraging women to take the place of men in industry. In 1918 the Representation of the People Act gave women over 30 the vote and this was extended to over 21s a decade later.

From Thomas Hedley to Proctor & Gamble

The Thomas Hedley Company had been trading in Newcastle for over ninety years when American firm Proctor & Gamble took it over in 1930. Hedley's was famous for producing Fairy Soap and the new company not only continued manufacturing this familiar nationwide brand but also introduced new lines such as Dreft and Tide. Soon their headquarters on City Road proved too small and they decided to build new offices at Gosforth.

The new complex was officially opened on 17th July 1953 by Major Gwilym Lloyd-George, Minister of Food and Newcastle North MP. Built on a nine acre green field site near South Gosforth Station a modern aspect of the new building was its use of large windows and glass dome rooflights allowing natural daylight to flood the offices and corridors. Another feature of sixty years

The landscaped Proctor & Gamble Gosforth Offices. Named Hedley House in honour of the Newcastle soapmaker, by 1962 the name of Thomas Hedley & Co had been changed to Proctor & Gamble.

ago that is taken for granted today was sound-proofing. Fibre-glass backed suspended ceilings and double-glazing helped absorb sound from within and from without.

One of the more unusual features of this post-war development was the inclusion of an air-raid shelter. On the advice of the Ministry of Works the basement of the new building was constructed of reinforced concrete allowing it to be adapted for use as an air-raid shelter. This was a time when the Cold War was at its height and the Korean War was in progress during the planning and construction of the building.

The 400 workers at Gosforth were well catered for with a waitress service restaurant and trolleys going round office to office serving tea and coffee at breaktimes. Outside of work activities were also provided on site with tennis courts, bowling green and a room for table tennis and darts.

In 2002 Proctor & Gamble closed its Gosforth Offices and relocated staff to various sites in this country and abroad. A housing development now occupies the site.

An advert for Thomas Hedley's most famous product a year before the Tyneside company was taken over by Proctor & Gamble.

The housing development built on the Proctor & Gamble site at the turn of the twenty-first century

Postcards from Gosforth

SANDRINGHAM ROAD So GOSFORTH 12

The postcard photographers of the early 1900s often took views of streets and these provide excellent historical images of how Gosforth looked around a hundred years ago. This was the heyday of the picture postcard when sending a card was as common as a text message or email today. Here is a postcard of Sandringham Road and it is a very peaceful view without a car in sight!

The following two postcards show The Grove. The card on the right is from around 1910. The houses in the foreground were fairly new when this photograph was taken, having been built around 1900. Numbers 32 to 36 and 38 to 52 of The Grove are Grade II listed.

The Grove, Gosforth. (166)

The Grove, Gosforth

Dear Olive, doesn't this road look pleasant I go this way to School. With Love From, Ethel.

The Grove from a postcard sent to an address in Forest Hall in 1903. The message on the front says: 'Dear Olive, doesn't this road look pleasant. I go this way to school. With love from Ethel.' People would post interesting cards to friends and family in the same way we post photographs on Facebook and other social media sites.

One day in the mid 1930s the Gateshead photographer and postcard publisher, Robert Johnston, visited Gosforth. Two of the photographs he took that day, one of Elmfield Road and the other of Linden Road, are on the right. Mr Johnston used a numbering system to catalogue his photographs and in the bottom left hand corner of these postcards are the numbers '8980' and '8981' so it is likely they were taken one after the other. Other photographs taken that day are on page 7 – 'High Street, Gosforth. 8976' – and page 9 – 'High Street, Gosforth. 8973'. Johnston was known for placing his car in his photographs – are any of the three cars in the postcards his?

Elmfield Road, Gosforth. 8980

Linden Road, Gosforth 8981

A very quiet Woodbine Avenue with only a dog around to pose for the postcard photographer in the early twentieth century. Around the time this photograph was taken, Woodbine Avenue was the home of William Bland a road contractor whose steam roller and workforce is featured on page 34.

A postcard showing a flood on the Great North Road in September 1913. A horse-drawn vehicle belonging to Provincial Laundries makes it way through the water. The company had laundries in South Gosforth, Whitley Bay and several in Newcastle. A gentleman has rolled up his trousers legs to cross the road.

Heavy rain that month caused chaos around Tyneside and Northumberland. The *Newcastle Journal* reported that during the thunderstorm: 'The atmosphere was so surcharged with electricity that many children and grown-up persons fainted.' The flooding on Tyneside brought out the postcard photographers and there are images that show the wet conditions at that time in Jesmond and Walker. Postcard publishers flocked to any form of disaster, natural or man-made and hundreds of cards were produced showing incidents such as tram and train crashes, Zeppelin bombing raids, mining accidents, shipwrecks and even landslides.

WEST AVENUE GOSFORTH

West Avenue with a couple of cyclists just visible in the distance. Today this street is lined with parked cars and seems much narrower than this view from the early 1900s. The young saplings in this postcard are now fully grown trees.

A view of Moor Crescent and, like a lot of postcards, children are posing for the photographer. On the right is the house 'Brookside' which was occupied in the early 1900s by Mr W. Crossling, a glass merchant. Today, this house still has ornate windows perhaps fitted by Mr Crossling.

MOOR CRESCENT, GOSFORTH.

ROTHWELL RD GOSFORTH

A postcard of Rothwell Road that was sent to Darlington in 1913. The message on the back reads: 'Cross denotes digs. I hope you are both A1. Love to both. Harry.' A few houses behind the boy in the road, a cross marks the spot where Harry was staying.

The driver and conductor of this number 20 tram take some time off at the Gosforth Park Gates terminus to have their photograph taken. Trams features in several of the postcards in this book. This one is off to Wallsend.

A picturesque postcard of the Avenue, Gosforth Park from the early 1900s. This is another postcard published by Robert Johnston of Gateshead.

Also available from Summerhill Books

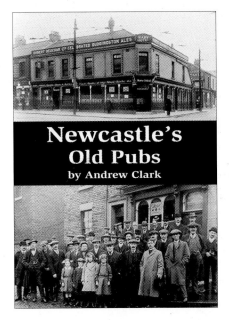

Summerhill Books publishes North East local history books. To receive a catalogue of our titles, send a stamped addressed envelope to:

Andrew Clark, Summerhill Books, PO Box 1210, Newcastle-upon-Tyne NE99 4AH

or email: summerhillbooks@yahoo.co.uk

or visit our website to view our full range of books: **www.summerhillbooks.co.uk**